EMOJI
COLORING BOOK

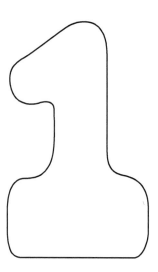

2

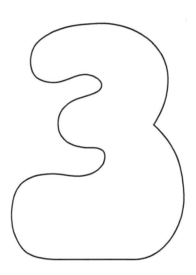

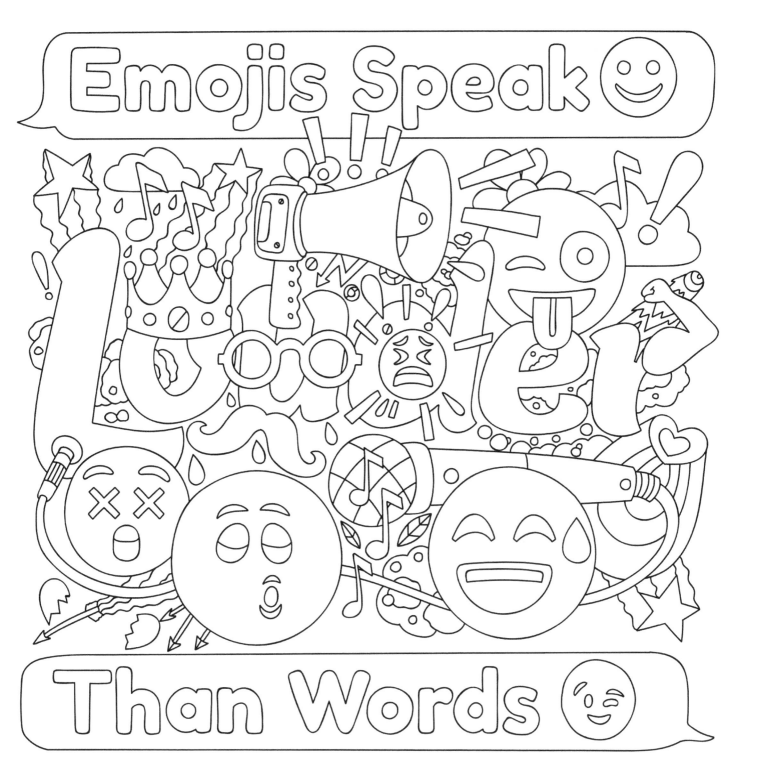

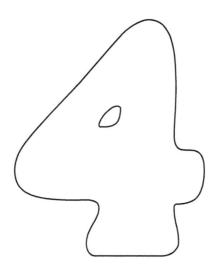

5

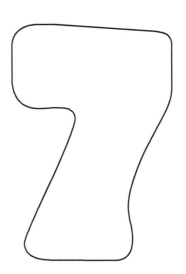

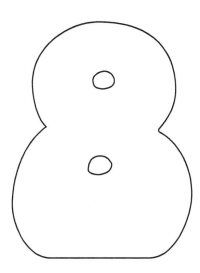

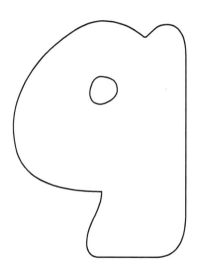

11

12

13

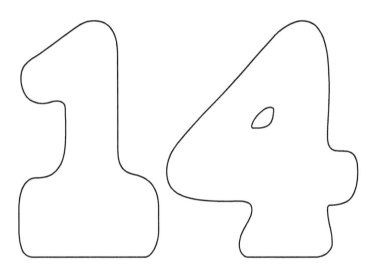

15

16

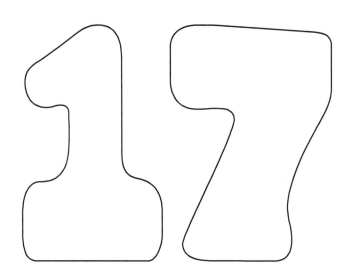

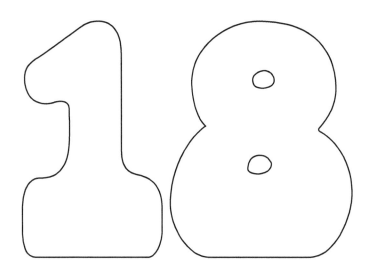

19

20

21

22

23

24

25

26

27

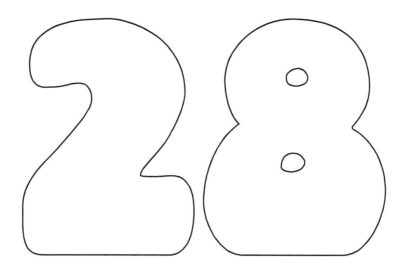

29

31

32

33

34

35

36

37

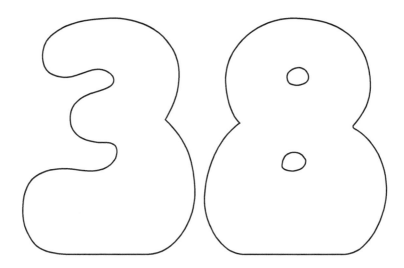

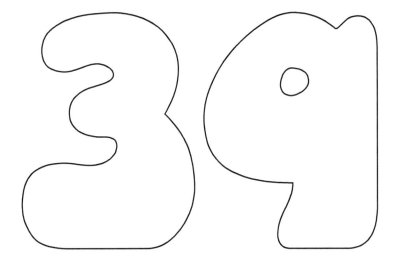

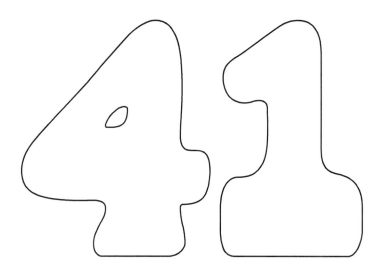

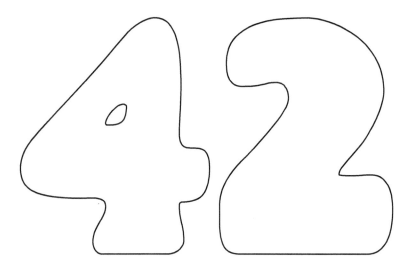

45

LIFE IS A DREAM

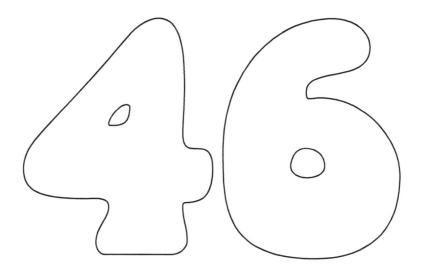

50

COLOR TEST PAGE

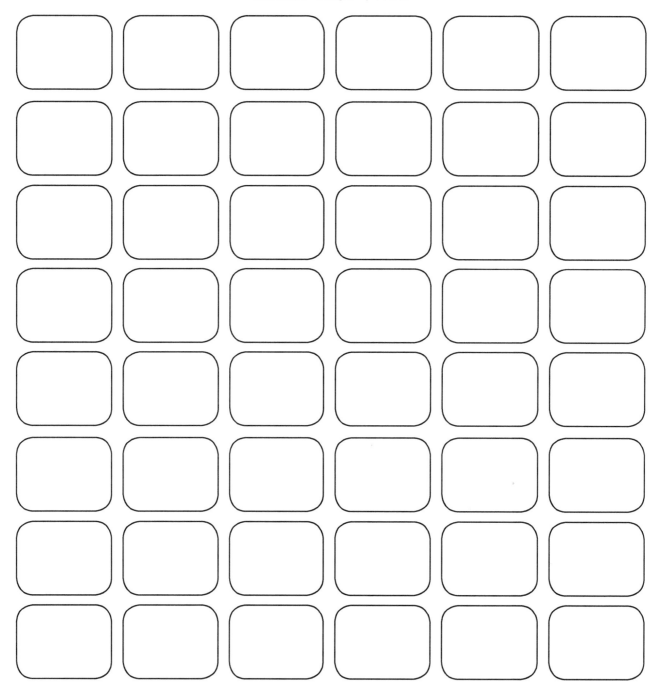

COLOR TEST PAGE

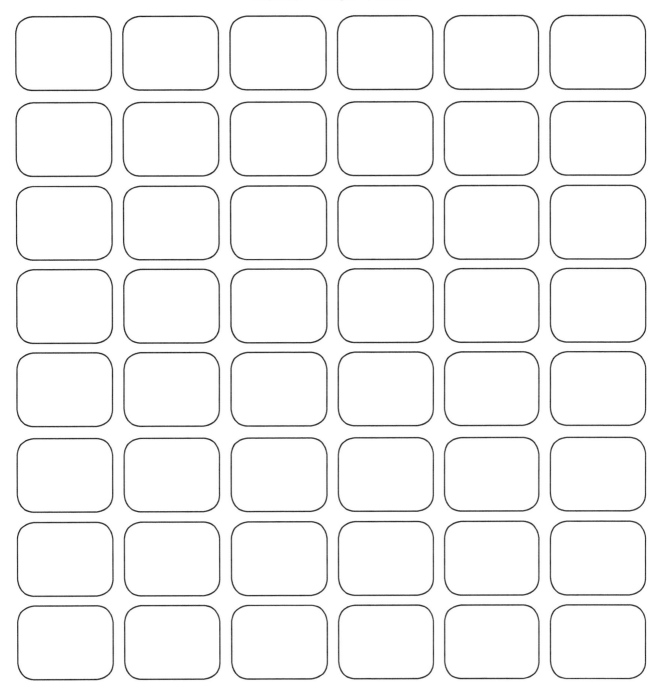

COLOR TEST PAGE

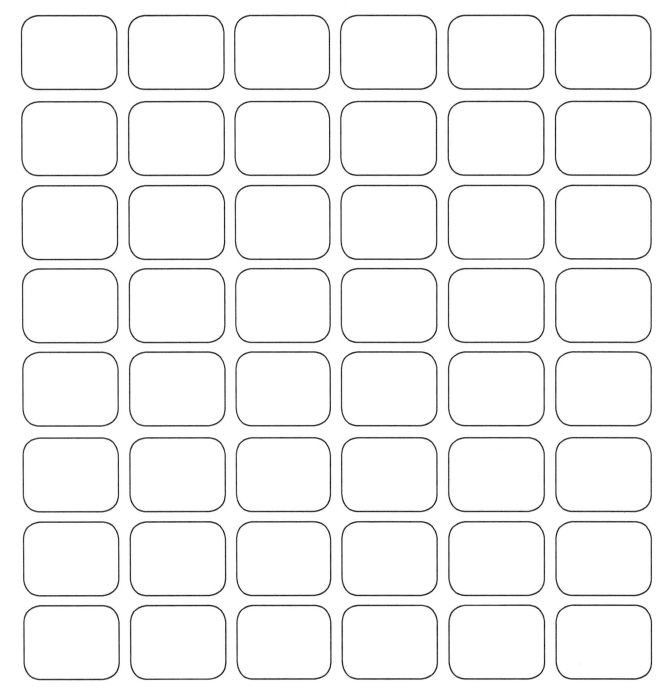

ONE LAST THING – WE WOULD LOVE TO HEAR YOUR FEEDBACK ABOUT THIS BOOK!

IF YOU FOUND THIS COLORING BOOK ENJOYABLE AND USEFUL, WE WOULD BE VERY GRATEFUL IF YOU POSTED A SHORT REVIEW ON AMAZON! YOUR SUPPORT DOES MAKE A DIFFERENCE AND WE READ EVERY REVIEW PERSONALLY.

IF YOU WOULD LIKE TO LEAVE A REVIEW, JUST HEAD ON OVER TO THIS BOOK'S AMAZON PAGE AND CLICK "WRITE A CUSTOMER REVIEW".

THANK YOU FOR YOUR SUPPORT!

www.ingramcontent.com/pod-product-compliance
Lightning Source LLC
LaVergne TN
LVHW060123070326

832902LV00019B/3114